BACKYARD SAFARI

Caterpillars and Butterflies

Trudi Strain Trueit

mc **Marshall Cavendish**
Benchmark
New York

Published by Marshall Cavendish Benchmark
An imprint of Marshall Cavendish Corporation

Website: www.marshallcavendish.us

This publication represents the opinions and views of the author based on Trudi Strain Trueit's personal experience, knowledge, and research. The information in this book serves as a general guide only. The author and publisher have used their best efforts in preparing this book and disclaim liability rising directly and indirectly from the use and application of this book.

Other Marshall Cavendish Offices:
Marshall Cavendish International (Asia) Private Limited, 1 New Industrial Road, Singapore 536196
Marshall Cavendish International (Thailand) Co Ltd. 253 Asoke, 12th Flr, Sukhumvit 21 Road, Klongtoey Nua, Wattana, Bangkok 10110, Thailand
Marshall Cavendish (Malaysia) Sdn Bhd, Times Subang, Lot 46, Subang Hi-Tech Industrial Park, Batu Tiga, 40000 Shah Alam, Selangor Darul Ehsan, Malaysia

Marshall Cavendish is a trademark of Times Publishing Limited

All websites were available and accurate when this book was sent to press.

Library of Congress Cataloging-in-Publication Data

Trueit, Trudi Strain.
Caterpillars and butterflies / by Trudi Strain Trueit.
p. cm. — (Backyard safari)
Summary: "Identify specific caterpillar and butterfly species. Explore their behavior, life cycle, mating habits, geographical location, anatomy, enemies, and defenses"—Provided by publisher.
Includes bibliographical references and index.
ISBN 978-1-60870-243-5 (print) ISBN 978-1-60870-625-9 (ebook)
1. Butterflies—Life cycles—Juvenile literature. 2. Butterflies—Identification—Juvenile literature. 3. Caterpillars—Juvenile literature. I. Title.
QL544.2.T774 2011
595.78'9—dc22
2010010018

Editor: Christine Florie
Publisher: Michelle Bisson
Art Director: Anahid Hamparian
Series Designer: Alicia Mikles

Expert Reader: Dr. Karen Oberhauser, University of Minnesota, Director, Monarchs in the Classroom

Photo research by Marybeth Kavanagh

Cover photo by *James Urbach/SuperStock*
The photographs in this book are used by permission and through the courtesy of: *Getty Images*: Lori Adamski Peek, 4; Darrell Gulin, 5; Paul Beard, 17 (top), 24E; Gail Shumway, 22 (top); *SuperStock*: Prisma, 6; age fotostock, 8, 13 (top), 22 (bottom), 23H, 24D, 24G, 28; Science Faction, 11; Purestock/H. Stanley Johnson, 15; Blend Images, 16; James Urbach, 23A, 23B, 23C, 23I, 23G, 24A, 24B; Mark Cassino, 24F; *Visuals Unlimited, Inc.*: Nigel Cattlin, 7 (top), *Animals Animals - Earth Scenes*: Patti Murray, 7 (bottom); *Alamy*: Keith Dannemiller, 9; Wayne Hutchinson, 23D; Rick & Nora Bowers, 23E; B. Mete Uz, 23F; B LaRue, 24H; Jeff Greenberg, 25; *Bill Trueit*: 10 , 24I; *Media Bakery*: BigStockPhoto, 13 (bottom right), 13 (bottom left), *Cutcaster*: Ivan Montero, 14B; Sergey Skryl, 14A; Marek Kosmal, 14C; Sergej Razvodovskij, 14D; *Envision*: Jean Higgins, 14 (bottom); PhotoEdit Inc.: Michael Newman, 17 (bottom); Dennis MacDonald, 27; *U.S. Fish and Wildlife Service*: Dr. Thomas G. Barnes, 24C

Printed in Malaysia (T)

1 3 5 6 4 2

Contents

Introduction

Have you ever watched baby spiders hatch from a silky egg sac? Or seen a butterfly sip nectar from a flower? If you have, you know how wonderful it is to discover nature for yourself. Each book in the Backyard Safari series will take you step-by-step on an easy outdoor adventure, then help you identify the animals you've found. You'll also learn ways to attract, observe, and protect these valuable creatures. As you read, be on the lookout for the Safari Tips and Trek Talk facts sprinkled throughout the book. Ready? The fun starts just steps from your back door!

ONE

Butterfly Basics

Whenever you see a butterfly zigzagging through your garden, you can't help but hope it will land on you! Butterflies are fascinating. They are part of a large order of insects called Lepidoptera (le-puh-DOP-tuh-ruh). It means "scaly wings." A butterfly's wings are covered with thousands of tiny scales. The scales overlap like tiles on a roof.

The scales of a swallowtail butterfly are seen through a high-powered microscope.

Safari Tip

When a butterfly's wings are touched, the "powder" that rubs off is its scales. It's not true that the insect cannot fly or will die if it loses some of its scales. Even so, it's not a good idea to handle a butterfly. Its thin wings can easily break. A damaged wing will never heal.

Did you ever wonder why you rarely see butterflies on a cool, cloudy day? A butterfly can't make enough body heat to warm its muscles for flight. Instead, it must **bask** in the Sun. It rests on a rock or a plant while its wings absorb heat. When a butterfly's body temperature reaches about 85 degrees Fahrenheit, it is ready to take off!

A swallowtail butterfly basks in the Sun. When it is warm enough, it will take flight.

Life in Motion

A butterfly goes through four stages of life: egg, **larva**, pupa (PYEW-puh), and adult.

Most adult females lay their eggs on the leaves of **host plants**. Each egg is about the size of a pinhead. It takes from a few days to a couple of weeks for eggs to hatch.

When it enters the world, a butterfly larva is an eating machine. It chews its way out of its egg, eats the shell, and usually begins munching on its host plant right away. It has powerful jaws. To grow, it molts, or sheds its skin. Caterpillars of most species molt four or five times during their first two weeks. By the end of that time, a caterpillar can weigh one thousand times more than it did at birth!

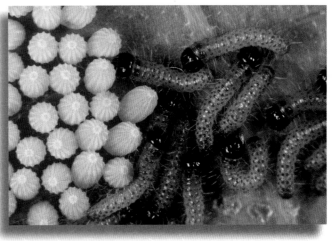

The laid eggs and hatched larvae of a large white butterfly are seen on the leaf of a host plant.

Trek Talk

Caterpillars such as this spring azure release a sweet liquid, or honeydew, that ants like to eat. In return, the ants protect the caterpillar from harm.

After a few weeks of nonstop growing, a caterpillar hangs upside down from a leaf or twig. The insect sheds its skin one last time to reveal a pupa, also called a **chrysalis** (KRI-suh-lus). Inside the chrysalis, a caterpillar's body begins to break down. Special cells rebuild it into a butterfly. How this occurs still puzzles scientists. The pupa stage lasts from one to two weeks for most species.

A monarch butterfly spends ten to fourteen days in its chrysalis before emerging as an adult.

An adult butterfly splits open its chrysalis. It struggles free. It pumps fluid from its abdomen into its wings. The fluid gives the wings shape. It takes about three hours for the wings to dry. Now the butterfly is ready to fly, feed, and mate. It must do all of these things quickly, because its life is short. Most butterflies live less than three weeks. A few, such as the monarch and mourning cloak, may live up to ten months.

Miraculous Monarchs

Each August, millions of monarch butterflies from Canada and the northern United States **migrate** for the winter. The monarchs ride the winds thousands of miles south to California or the mountains of central Mexico. It is spectacular to see large groups of butterflies clustered on a single fir tree! The next February, the monarchs begin the trip home. However, they do not live to complete it. The females lay their eggs on milkweed plants as they fly north. Then they die. It's up to the generations that follow to continue the flight home. Year after year, monarchs migrate to the same place their ancestors did. How do they know where to go? Somehow they just do!

Sensitive Beauty

An adult butterfly weighs about as much as a paper clip, yet it has powerful senses. A butterfly has excellent eyesight. Each large eye is made up of thousands of lenses. For humans, it would be like looking at the world through a giant honeycomb. However, scientists believe butterflies see a single image. These compound eyes allow the butterfly to look in every direction at once. Butterflies see the same colors humans do, plus some colors we are not able to see. This sharp eyesight helps them find their favorite flowers.

A butterfly has a pair of hind wings, a pair of front wings, and six legs.

Butterflies have six legs. Each leg has a pair of claws, or tarsi. The tarsi allow the insect to climb and cling to perches. Tiny hairs on the tarsi are used for tasting. These hairs are so sensitive, they can detect sugar at two hundred times lower than the amount a human can taste! An adult butterfly no longer has the strong jaws it did as a caterpillar. To eat, it uncurls a long, tonguelike organ called a proboscis (pruh-BAH-sus or pruh-BAHS-kus). It is a tube like a drinking straw. The proboscis is used to sip the nectar (juice) from flowers, fruit, and vegetables. Some butterflies may feed on tree sap, tears, or animal droppings. Male butterflies will often puddle, or sip salt water from wet or sandy soil. The salt gives them extra nutrients.

Now that you've had a glimpse into the ever-changing world of butterflies, it's time to go on safari!

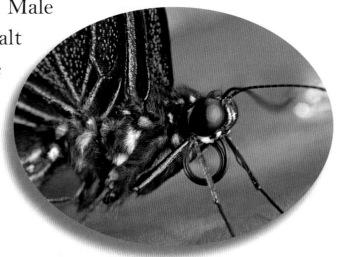

When this butterfly is ready to eat, it will uncurl its proboscis.

TWO

You Are
the Explorer

Butterfly watching can be exciting. Perhaps you'll get a close-up view of a caterpillar transforming into a chrysalis. Or discover two butterflies swirling in a mating dance. On the other hand, you might not see much at all. That's all right. A butterfly safari takes time, patience, and a little luck. No matter what happens on your safari, if you take a friend along, you're sure to have fun.

You will increase your chance of success if you pick a sunny day between May and early October to go on safari. If you choose a crisp, clear morning, you are more likely to find butterflies basking. It should be fairly easy to take pictures of them while they rest. If you go later in the day when temperatures are above 60 °F, you'll probably see more butterflies (they will be warm enough to fly). However, active butterflies are also harder to photograph.

Why Do We Call Them Butterflies?

It most likely started with the male brimstone butterfly (right). Hundreds of years ago, people in Great Britain referred to this large, yellow insect as a butter-colored fly, which became butterfly.

What Do I Wear?

* A hat with a brim
* A long-sleeved shirt
* Jeans or long pants
* Sunglasses
* Sunscreen

Safari Tip

Rather than risk injuring a butterfly by picking it up, try this: put on a solid purple, white, or yellow shirt or hat. These are the colors of the flowers that butterflies are most attracted to. By wearing their favorite shades, you are inviting them to land on you!

What Do I Take?

* Binoculars (a pair that focuses within 15 feet is best)
* Digital camera
* Magnifying glass
* Notebook
* Colored pens or pencils
* Water

Where Do I Go?

Find a place in your backyard that is attractive to butterflies. They will be looking for:

* Flowers to feed on (caterpillars will be eating the leaves of plants and trees)
* Rocks to bask on
* Plants to bask, mate, and lay their eggs on
* Water to drink (birdbath, mud puddle, or wet rocks)

This garden contains many favorite things of butterflies, such as flowers, rocks, and water.

If your backyard doesn't offer these features, here are some other good safari locations:

- ❋ Meadows
- ❋ Open woodlands
- ❋ Wetlands
- ❋ Fields
- ❋ Public parks
- ❋ Garden nurseries

Always have an adult with you if you are going beyond your backyard.

Playing Keep Away

Some swallowtail caterpillars (right) have **eyespots**, body markings that are meant to trick **predators** into thinking the caterpillar is a snake. Swallowtail caterpillars also have a forked gland called an **osmeterium** (ohz-muh-TIR-ee-um). When the insect is threatened, the osmeterium pops out from behind the caterpillar's head like a snake's tongue. It releases a strong, citrus odor that may startle predators. (It's not harmful to humans.)

What Do I Do?

❋ Choose a sunny spot next to some flowers, if possible.

❋ Take a good look around. There's no need to rush. Scan the area with your binoculars. Do you spy a butterfly resting on a rocky path? Drinking dew from a petal?

❋ Use your magnifying glass to check for chrysalides and caterpillars on the tops and bottoms of leaves. Look carefully! Some caterpillars have good **camouflage**.

Safari Tip

It's usually okay to hold a caterpillar, though those with spines can cause a minor skin rash in some people. Just be gentle with the tiny crawler and let it go after a few minutes. Also, place it back exactly where you found it. Caterpillars are picky eaters, and many will eat only their host plant.

You can get an up-close look at a butterfly, caterpillar, or chrysalis by using your magnifying glass.

Trek Talk
The dogface is named for the outline of a dog's head that marks each forewing. Can you find one?

* Snap photos or make sketches of the insects you find.

* Take notes on your discoveries. For a caterpillar, write down its colors and markings. Do you see eyespots or camouflage markings? How about the caterpillar's **texture**? Is it spiny or smooth? For a butterfly, look at its wings. How are they shaped? Do the hind wings have tips? What about colors and patterns? Most likely, the tops will look different from the undersides. If you only get a brief glimpse of a butterfly's top wing colors, that's okay. You should still be able to identify it later.

Be sure to take notes of your findings, writing down colors, markings, size, shape, and so on. You will use them later to help identify the caterpillars and butterflies you saw.

❊ As you make notes, draw a line at the bottom of each entry for the butterfly's name (you'll fill that in later).

❊ Make a drawing of your insect beside its entry or leave space to paste in a photo.

BUTTERFLY

Wing colors: white, black

Markings: zebra stripes, tiny red and blue spots on hind wings

Wings: long, thin tails on hind wings

Insect name: _____

Your Drawing or Photo Goes Here

CATERPILLAR

Colors: white, black, yellow

Markings: stripes

Texture: smooth

Insect name: _____

Your Drawing or Photo Goes Here

* Spend about a half hour to an hour on safari (don't forget to drink your water).
* Clean up the area and take everything with you when you leave.

Now that your safari is finished, did you get some great photographs or see something new? Congratulations! If not, don't get discouraged. Plan another safari soon. Every expedition is different. Who knows what you'll discover next time?

At home, download your photos onto the computer and print them. Grab your photos and notebook. Move on to the next chapter. It's time to learn more about your backyard visitors!

THREE

A Guide to Caterpillars and Butterflies

You've had a busy day trekking through your backyard jungle. Now it's time to try to identify the insects you've found. Compare your photos, drawings, and notes to the pictures of the caterpillars and butterflies on the following pages. Here's how to do it:

To identify a caterpillar, try to match the color and texture. Ask yourself:

* Does it have one color or many colors?
* Does it have stripes, eyespots, or camouflage markings?
* Is it covered in spines or is it smooth?

Note: if your caterpillar has a thick coat of fuzzy fur, it's probably a moth.

To identify a butterfly, focus on matching color and wing shape. Ask yourself:

- ❊ What are its main wing colors?
- ❊ What are the markings on the wings?
- ❊ How are the wings shaped? Do the tails have tips?

There are more than seven hundred known types of butterflies in North America—far too many to picture here. Still, we've grouped butterflies by family, so even if you don't find an exact match you should be able to tell which of the major families your butterfly belongs to:

- ❊ Swallowtails
- ❊ Whites and Sulphurs
- ❊ Brush-footed
- ❊ Skippers

Once you've identified your insect(s), go back and write its name in your notebook. Also, if you took photographs, paste them in your notebook, too.

BUTTERFLY

Wing colors: white, black

Markings: zebra stripes, tiny red and

blue spots on hind wings

Wings: long, thin tails on hind wings

Insect name: ZEBRA SWALLOWTAIL

CATERPILLAR

Colors: white, black, yellow

Markings: stripes

Texture: smooth

Insect name: MONARCH

Caterpillars

Compare your photos or drawings to the photos of the caterpillars on the next page. If you find a match, flip ahead to the butterfly guide on page 24 to see what the caterpillar will look like as an adult!

Caterpillar Guide

SWALLOWTAILS

Black Swallowtail

Zebra Swallowtail

Tiger Swallowtail

WHITES AND SULPHURS

Cabbage White

Dogface

SKIPPERS

Silver-spotted Skipper

BRUSH-FOOTED

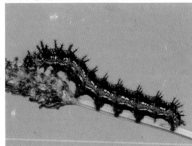

Buckeye

Painted Lady

Zebra Longwing

Butterfly Guide

SWALLOWTAILS

Black Swallowtail

Zebra Swallowtail

Tiger Swallowtail

WHITES AND SULPHURS

Cabbage White

Dogface

SKIPPERS

Silver-spotted Skipper

BRUSH-FOOTED

Buckeye

Painted Lady

Zebra Longwing

FOUR

Try This!
Projects You Can Do

Butterflies are important to our world. They pollinate plants, which give us fruits and seeds. Yet the forests, meadows, and fields that butterflies depend on are disappearing. Humans are clearing them for growth. When you do these projects, you are helping butterflies have a brighter future.

Butterfly Garden

It's easy to plant a small garden that will attract butterflies. Choose six to eight plants from the Butterfly Favorites Plant List on page 26. Select plants from both categories: host plants and nectar plants. This will help to keep the butterfly life cycle going. It also keeps more butterflies in your yard, because you are giving them what they need to survive. The butterflies we've listed

Once you've chosen plants that attract butterflies, choose a sunny spot to create a butterfly garden in your own yard.

are common throughout North America. With a little research, you can find out about specific butterflies that live in your area and which plants they prefer. Contact your garden nursery or check the web resources at the back of this book for more information.

Pick a sunny spot for your garden that is out of the wind. Use good soil. Add a few large, flat rocks for basking. Water your garden every few days (the damp soil and rocks will also lure butterflies in for a drink). Never use pesticides. Enjoy your butterflies and blooms!

Butterfly Favorites Plant List

BUTTERFLY TYPE	HOST PLANTS (CATERPILLARS)	NECTAR PLANTS (ADULTS)
cabbage and most whites	mustards, cabbage, broccoli	lavender, heliotrope
alfalfa and most sulphurs	clover, lupine	clover, thistle, zinnia
giant swallowtail	citrus, prickly ash	lantana, butterfly bush
American painted lady	daisy	daisy, yarrow, heliotrope
buckeye	snapdragon, verbena	clover, cosmos, Indian blanket
monarch	milkweed	daisy, aster, zinnia

Create your own butterfly fruit plate. See how many kinds of butterflies stop by for a sip.

Butterfly Fruit Plate

The nectar from rotting fruit is a favorite among many butterflies, including mourning cloak, comma, and question mark. Just about any fruit will draw them in: melons, peaches, apples, oranges, bananas, strawberries. Choose a fruit or two. Have an adult help you slice it into small chunks and arrange it on a plastic plate. On a sunny day, place the plate outside in a shady area off the ground. A windowsill, deck railing, or sturdy tree branch will do. If you're lucky, you may get a winged visitor or two! Throw out the fruit at the end of the day so you don't attract rodents at night.

Trek Talk
Birds often mistake the buckeye's eyespots for an owl and will leave the butterfly alone.

Watering Station

Provide water for thirsty butterflies in the heat of summer. Find an old rubber car mat or welcome mat. Place it in a sunny location in your backyard (next to flowers, if possible). Soak it with a garden hose. That's it! You may have to dampen the mat several times throughout the afternoon. You'll be surprised at how many butterflies stop in for a drink on a hot day.

Butterflies are fragile, yet strong. Plentiful, yet precious. Mysterious, yet carefree. Perhaps that is why when one flits past we must stop to watch. We know we are seeing something special. We are seeing nature's magic.

Glossary

bask　　　　　to soak up heat from the Sun

camouflage　　to use color as a disguise

chrysalis　　　a butterfly's hard pupa covering

eyespots　　　camouflage markings on a caterpillar or adult butterfly

host plant　　the plant on which a female butterfly chooses to lay her eggs that becomes food for the newborn caterpillars

larva　　　　　caterpillar

migrate　　　to move from one region to another with the changing seasons

osmeterium　a forklike organ located behind the head of a swallowtail caterpillar used for protection against predators

predators　　animals that hunt other animals for food

texture　　　the feel of a surface

Find Out More

Books

Goldish, Meish. *Beautiful Butterflies.* New York: Bearport, 2008.

Nelson, Sara Elizabeth. *Butterflies.* Minneapolis, MN: Lerner, 2008.

Rustad, Martha E. H. *Butterflies.* Minneapolis, MN: Bellwether Media, 2008.

DVDs

Butterflies and Moths. DK Eyewitness, 2007.

The Story of the Butterfly. Janson Media, 2007.

Websites

Butterflies and Moths of North America

www.butterfliesandmoths.org

Scientists from the U.S. Geological Survey's Northern Prairie Wildlife Research Center designed this informative website. Check out the photo gallery to see hundreds of butterflies from around the world.

The Butterfly Conservation Initiative

www.butterflyrecovery.org

Learn more about the butterflies that live in your area and how to attract them. At this site you can also find a butterfly garden or exhibit to visit that is near you.

Monarch Butterfly Journey North

www.learner.org/jnorth/monarch

Track monarchs as they migrate each fall and spring. If you live along a migration route, you can even report your monarch sightings.

Index

Page numbers in **boldface** are illustrations.

About the Author

TRUDI STRAIN TRUEIT has been fascinated with butterflies since she was a kid growing up in the Pacific Northwest. An award-winning television news reporter and anchor, she has written more than fifty fiction and nonfiction books for children. Her titles cover everything from storm chasing to video gaming. She is the author of four other books in the Backyard Safari series, including *Birds, Spiders,* and *Squirrels.* Trudi lives near Seattle, Washington, with her husband, Bill, a photographer, who took some of the butterfly photos featured in this book. Bill and Trudi go butterfly watching whenever they can! Find out more about them at www.truditrueit.com and www.billtrueit.com.